STOP STEVEN, STOP

...the angel yelled chasing after him.

STOP STEVEN, STOP

...the angel yelled
chasing after him.

DR. SUSAN MARIE PENDER

Christian International Publishing
Santa Rosa Beach, Florida

Dr. Susan Marie Pender
www.rebuildinglives.net

Christian International Publishing
177 Apostles Way
Santa Rosa Beach, Florida 32459
www.cipublishing.org

This book or parts thereof may not be reproduced in any form stored in a retrieval system, or transmitted in any form by any means—electronic, mechanical, photocopy, recording or otherwise—without proper written permission of the publisher, except as provided by United States of America copyright law.

All scripture quotations, unless otherwise indicated, are from the *Holy Bible Thompson Chain-Reference Bible* New International Version Copyright 1990 by The B.B. Kirkbride Bible Company, Inc. Indianapolis, Indiana.

Copyright 2018 by Susan Pender. All rights reserved

Thank you Rebecca Francis and Sally Saxon for editing this book and for your hearts of compassion.

ISBN: 978-1-7325703-0-6
Published August 2018
Printed in the United States of America

DEDICATION

I would like to thank my Lord and Savior Jesus Christ for loving me and drawing me to Him with His kindness. I would have been lost in this world and for all of eternity if He had not paid my debt of sin and won my heart. Thank you, Father God, for giving me provision, keeping me safe, and never withdrawing Your plans from my life or giving up on me. Thank you Holy Spirit for walking with me, giving me counsel, comfort, and for using me in prayer. I never want to be without You.

I would like to dedicate this writing to all the families who have lost a loved one to a premature death related to alcohol or drugs. There is a brokenness in the hearts of these families. God wants to restore us and our families.

ENDORSEMENT

"I must say this is one of the most sensitive and heartfelt stories I have ever read. Susan has taken a tragic life event that would devastate even the most hardened of hearts and told of how God can take you from tragedy to triumph. This is a must read, not only for those who have suffered loss but for anyone who wishes to understand and help those who have. God has given Susan deep insight into how to navigate your way through dark trials to His shining Light and Peace."

Pastor Missy Marcinkowski
Family Pastor, Vision Church @ Christian International

CONTENTS

Prophetic Word	i
Introduction	iii
1: Hurting Inside	1
2: The Angel Cried, "Stop Steven, Stop"	9
3: Holy Spirit Intercedes Through Us	15
4: Decisions Can Mean Life or Death	21
5: God Does Intervene In Our Lives	27
6: My Broken-Hearted Condition	31
7: Grieving Causes Health Issues	37
8: Trauma and Grief	41
9: Crying Out For Answers	45
10: Turn it Around	53
Endnotes	59
Bibliography	61
More from the Author	63

PROPHETIC WORD

November 4, 2015, given by Pastor Priscilla from Tallahassee, Florida to Susan Pender.

Do you have a son named Steven? Daughter the pain you felt and the loss you had and the trauma you went through, I am going to redeem that. I will have you share your past concerning that area of trauma. I want you to share with other people what happened to Steven and that loss you suffered, that trauma you felt. I want you to help them through their trauma.

DEFINITION OF A PROPHETIC WORD

A prophetic word according to 1 Corinthians 14:1, 3: "Follow the way of love and eagerly desire spiritual gifts, especially the gift of prophecy. Everyone who prophesies speaks to men for their strengthening, encouragement, and comfort."

Also in 2 Peter 1:20, 21: "Above all, you must understand that no prophecy of Scripture came about by the prophet's own interpretation. For prophecy never had its origin in the will of man, but men spoke from God as they were carried along by the Holy Spirit."

According to Dr. Bill Hamon, pioneer of the Prophetic Movement in the late 1980s, this is the definition of a prophetic word: "God's revelation of His thoughts and intents to a particular person, family, or group of people. It is specific information coming from the mind of God for a specific situation, an inspired word directed to a certain audience."[1]

INTRODUCTION

Children are a gift and a blessing from the Lord. Psalm 127:3, "Sons are a heritage from the Lord, children a reward from him." Nothing is more valuable in a home than these. Many wealthy people would give all they have to hear the cry of a baby born to them. Nothing was of more value to me than being in a family, the one I grew up in, and later having one of my own. Family was God's idea.

Family has always been the most important thing in my life. Living in a family allows us to learn how to work and play together. This is where we learn to forgive and to love one another. It is also where we learn to be in a relationship with one another. Family sits together and talks about their lives together; what is currently happening, and what they are planning for their future.

I never planned for or even thought about divorce. I prayed for my husband in the privacy of my room for many years that he would fulfill his role as a husband and as a father, and at his workplace, and that he would be content in his life. I prayed that he would have peace in his heart, be kind, and have a relationship with the Lord. If a family does not attend church and school functions together, have mutual friends and attend social functions with each other, there is little holding them together.

At the time we divorced, our children were 8, 9, and 12 years old. I bought a home in a small neighboring town to lower my expenses. I had only $1,000 after 23 years of marriage. I didn't know how I would manage my financial obligations alone and couldn't foresee how I could continue on without lowering my expenses. I worked a full-time job as a nurse for an insurance company, had a second part-time job as a nurse on the weekends, and also had a third seasonal employment during the months of September and October. I didn't have a cell phone or the ability to make long-distance phone calls, nor did I have cable television or any such conveniences because of my low-income status.

Relocating to my hometown seemed like the best decision so my young children could grow up among their cousins. I felt it would give them and myself a sense of belonging while being close to my family. Yet there were many unforeseen difficulties that arose in my home after divorce; settling of legal issues, children changing schools, parents changing jobs, other family members adjusting to our new situation, living in a different city, moving to a different home, disagreements between parents, ongoing communication problems, etc. These all stress the members of the household. I did the best I knew how in coping with this life transition and caring for my home, but we all suffered painful emotions.

I know God heard and saw everything experienced in my home whether it was joy or sadness and whether it was right or wrong. Proverb 5:21 says "For a man's ways are in full view of the Lord, and he examines all his paths." Through all the difficulties, I know God was with us: "So do not fear, for I am with you; do not be dismayed, for I am your God. I will strengthen you and help you; I will uphold you with my righteous right hand." (Isaiah 41:10). Most people will experience major difficulties in their lifetime, but God still promises to be there to help us if we call upon Him. The most difficult situation I have had to cope with was my own child's overdose.

Having a child or teenager die of a drug or alcohol overdose, whatever the situation or circumstance may be, causes a brokenness in the hearts of those close to them. I found through this experience that my child's life did not escape without being noticed by a loving, caring Father God. I will share the things that helped me see God reaching out through it all. The hearts that are left crushed do not go unnoticed either. Psalm 147:3 says, "He heals the brokenhearted and binds up their wounds." Psalm 34:18 says, "The Lord is close to the brokenhearted and saves those who are crushed in spirit."

There is hope for everyone who has gone through

a similar situation as mine. God sustained me through this painful time and He continues to do a work of restoration in me. I know He wants to help you too.

one
HURTING INSIDE

My youngest son Steven was approximately 13 or 14 years old when he began using alcohol. I was cleaning his bedroom when I first found a container of alcohol among his clothes. I knew he was having difficulty in school and was not completing his homework on time. I recognized that he was acting more withdrawn, which was not his normal personality. Eventually, he did not want to participate in sports and other activities that previously interested him. I realized his problems were not just school related but went much deeper. Unknowingly, I thought if I get rid of the alcohol, my son would be all right. I never thought he might be using some form of a chemical also. It wasn't until much later that I suspected he was using these and would search out the true nature of his personality changes.

As time went on his school classes became more difficult for him. He was having failing grades. His behavior did not improve and his personality was becoming increasingly different from who he had been. He became more distant and argumentative. He would come home after dark and not always get up for school in the mornings. Often I went to work long before my children got up to prepare for school and then get themselves off to school. I would follow-up with them by calling home to verify they were all right and able to leave for school on time.

With all of the negative signs in Steven's behavior, I suspected that he may be using some kind of drug. I don't know if I was just denying that my son had a drug problem or if I was so distracted in my own responsibilities at work and with college courses I was taking to improve my financial situation that I wasn't able to see sooner what was happening to him. Neither his school nor any teachers notified me that they suspected he had an addiction to drug or alcohol, only that his grades were dropping. He would deny he was using any chemicals, but his drastic change in behavior revealed something different.

Finally, I purchased an online drug test kit. I was able to obtain from him what I needed for this test one particular evening when he came home late. Using this kit, I could then identify the chemicals he was using. By this time Steven's weight had visibly dropped to where he was noticeably thin. This test kit gave a positive result of the precise chemicals and amounts in his system. I had a sense of relief just knowing the truth.

I let Steven see what the results were on this drug test. He almost seemed relieved that he didn't have to hide this from me any longer. I told him I would search out the possibilities available for him to receive some kind of drug counseling. He agreed and wanted help. The county connected us to a drug counseling program that would allow him to continue his high school education. I talked with Steven about this program and he readily acknowledged that he needed help. He consented to go to Northland Recovery in Grand Rapids, Minnesota. This was a two-month program. He could continue his high school education there. He got into this program almost immediately. They allowed family to visit him at this facility only on weekends. We could also write letters. There were no family counseling sessions offered at this facility.

I had taken part in an alcohol treatment program with my father years before this and was actively involved in the family counseling that took place at that time. In this facility at Northland Recovery, there was no family counseling. The family could only visit at certain hours on weekends. After this in-patient counseling and education, Steven returned home. When he returned home, he also returned to the same school and the same environment. By this time, I was working just one full-time job close to our home so I could be more available. But it wasn't long until I suspected that he was using drugs again.

Steven had a tenderness and gentleness about him. He had a wonderful sense of humor, which added so much to our home. He had many friends and especially had compassion for those disabled or looked down upon. He wasn't one to judge anyone or ever talk bad about anyone. He had a delightful sense of humor, and he was a really fun person to be around.

One day when he came home from school, I could see he had been crying. As I sat in his bedroom with him, I asked him what had happened. He related how one of his friends was having a hard time in school. He told me his friend's dad lived in another state and had recently committed suicide. Steven saw the difficulty his friend was having in school and was crying over the loss and sadness his friend was feeling. Steven may have identified with his friend's grief.

In reading books about addictions, along with my own life experiences in my family, I came to believe the root cause of alcohol and drug use is feeling unloved. Even if we are brought up in a good home with everything we need whether one parent or both parents are present, people can still feel unloved. How much more my children must have felt unloved because of the stress of constant legal actions between their father and I and the frequent lack of a parent in the home. I believe my son found an emotional relief to the stresses around him by using a 'painkiller' called meth, alcohol, cocaine and whatever kind of drug he could get.

Steven had aspirations of playing college football with the Titans. He had dreams of being a world-renowned fisherman on television. Then later he expressed a desire to attend college to be an addiction counselor. He was interested in going to college for addiction counseling even though at that time in his life he wasn't free of the addictions himself.

In 2005 he was arrested for stealing and having drugs in his possession. After a court hearing, instead of sending him to prison, the judge allowed him to be admitted to an addiction treatment center at Thistledew Correctional Facility in Cook, Minnesota. This was a three-month rehabilitation program. This facility didn't offer family counseling and allowed limited contact. Writing letters, sending packages, and minimal scheduled phone calls were all the contact I had with Steven. He could also exchange letters with his siblings.

During this time I sent him several books to read, specifically choosing ones about David Wilkerson and Nicky Cruz. I thought these books would encourage him. David Wilkerson risked his life ministering on the streets of New York. He helped many who were addicted to drugs by sharing the love of God in a tangible way. One such gang member was Nicky Cruz. Nicky Cruz as a young man was the leader of a New York City gang called the Mau-Maus. He lived on the streets of New York with others who used alcohol and drugs. They would steal from people or from stores to purchase their food and their drugs to support their lifestyle.

Nicky gave his life to the Lord after a radical encounter with God's love, a message Nicky had never heard before this time. With help from David Wilkerson, Nicky and several others took in addicts and provided them with food and shelter. They would pray immediately for the addicted person until they were completely free from the withdrawal symptoms of the drugs they had used. They shared God's love with them until they accepted Jesus Christ as their savior. Then they prayed with them to receive the Baptism of the Holy Spirit, they testified that the addicts who received the Baptism of the Holy Spirit had a much higher rate of living a life free of drug use. This was the beginning of the program called, "Teen Challenge."

I scheduled my first visit with Steven at this Thistledew Correctional Facility towards the end of his third month. We were to discuss with Steven and his two counselors where he would live after being released from this facility. No one else went with me. It was a six-hour drive from where I lived. It was so wonderful to see him. He looked healthier and had gained his normal weight back.

After some pleasant conversation about how much the counselors enjoyed Steven and light discussion on how much Steven had progressed, we discussed Steven's living arrangements when he returned home. We decided Steven would be coming home to live with me and his two other siblings. He would attend a different school this time, located in Moorhead, Minnesota. This school was for students with prior drug-related problems. In a couple weeks, I would return to the Thistledew facility for his graduation, and then we would come home together.

Upon returning home that evening, I immediately searched out a different place for us to live. I did not want Steven returning to my home and living in the same environment again. I looked for a parcel of land to move my mobile home onto that was in a different community. I just happened to share with my father in conversation that I would move somewhere else just so I was not in the same town and the same environment. My father offered me a parcel of his land that I could move my home onto. This was in the country, away from the small town where I lived. I could not move there until October, over a month after Steven returned home.

The plans were such that Steven would attend a different school for teens with a history of drug use in a neighboring city. I scheduled a driver to come to our home to pick him up along with one other student and then drive them to-and-from school each day. Within the first month of school, Steven was not getting up to meet his ride. He could not stop using drugs. He never did move with me to the new location of my home. Instead, he moved to Fargo, North Dakota to live with his father. There he got a job at a fast-food restaurant. Shortly after that he acquired his GED (diploma).

two

THE ANGEL CRIED, "STOP STEVEN, STOP"

In August 2006, I received a phone call from Steven. He asked if I could help him find another treatment facility, adding the words, "really soon and one that really works this time." After I ended my day at work, I picked him up at his sister's apartment in Moorhead where he was visiting for the day. I planned to take him home with me to discuss treatment options with him.

When I arrived to pick him up, I could see that something upset him. He was visibly shaken. He was to the point of sobbing yet wanting to verbalize what he had just experienced. He got in the car with me and looked like he was trying to get his thoughts together to share with me what had disturbed him. Steven asked me to keep driving the car and just listen. So I drove slowly while listening to what he had to say. He gathered his thoughts and began to verbalize what had just happened to him.

Steven said he was walking outside his sister's apartment, then hesitated to collect his thoughts, and continued telling me what had happened. While he was walking along down the sidewalk outside his sister's apartment, he heard someone yelling at him by name saying, "Stop Steven, Stop!" This frightened him because he didn't see anyone around, so he jogged down the sidewalk. This voice chased after him and continued yelling at him, "Stop Steven, Stop!" He said he knew it was an angel.

This upset Steven. He cried some as he shared this with me because of the reality that God was intervening in his life. He tried to find words to explain this to me. I kept slowly driving my car as he struggled to compose himself and relate what happened. I believed he had heard an angel because I had seen and experienced angels at different times in my life as well. Yet I didn't know what more to say about his experience. I listened and supported the reality that God had sent an angel to speak clearly to warn him to stop using drugs. Psalm 91:11 says, "For He will command his angels concerning you to guard you in all your ways." This was one reason he had called me on my cell phone to ask for help in locating a good treatment facility "really soon."

When we arrived at my home, we talked about the places we knew that he could go for addiction treatment again. Our knowledge for help was very limited, and he kept reiterating he wanted something different, something that "really worked." A friend told him about a place in Arizona, but he had no information about it. I didn't know how I would get him there or how I could help him when I was living so far away. I was familiar with a place in Pennsylvania and called to inquire about availability and financial requirements. These both quickly became closed doors. The next day I took him back to his father's home in Fargo, North Dakota and went to my workplace. I said I would search for a good place to get help.

While at work I thought about the possibility of enrolling Steven in a Teen Challenge facility. I called several Teen Challenge facilities in four different states before I found one that had an immediate opening. It was in South Dakota. Steven only had to sign the application. He was an adult at 18 years of age, so had to make his own decision whether or not to sign the application.

I immediately called Steven to ask if he could meet with me after I got off work that day. I told him about the Teen Challenge facility in South Dakota and that they had an opening for him. He was willing to meet with me and hear about this facility. We met in the parking lot at the Barnes and Noble Bookstore in Fargo.

After I got off work, I drove to this parking lot. Steven was there waiting for me. He planned to meet with some of his friends at a restaurant nearby after visiting with me. As we sat in my car, I shared with him that I talked to the director at a Teen Challenge facility in South Dakota, and they had an opening for him. They agreed to hold this opening for Steven, allowing him 24 hours to secure his placement with them. Steven only needed to call the director on the phone and accept being admitted.

I handed Steven a piece of paper with the director's phone number on it so he could call them and accept being admitted. I reminded him that this was a year-long program, and their success rate was very high. I told him they study the Bible in their recovery program.

Steven was quiet while thinking about what I shared. Then he said he was not going to attend church for the next year of his life. He got out of my car, shut the door, and went with his friends.

At that time, I heard inside of me a still, small voice say, "He doesn't want to spend the next year of his life in church, but he will spend eternity in heaven." This thought came to me so quickly. I knew it could not have originated from my mind. I didn't have time to even process what Steven had just said and then generate a response because he left my car so quickly and abruptly.

For the last two days, he had asked me to help him find a place to get help, "really soon." He seemed to be desperate. But now, he turned down an opportunity for help that was only a phone call away. Even though I was shocked at his negative response and deeply saddened that he didn't take this opportunity offered to him, I felt a sense of relief in hearing the words "he will be in heaven for eternity" someday. I felt assurance that he was going to be all right somehow and that he would have a long, successful life. I reasoned that no matter what, Steven would be okay.

I knew Steven's choices were out of my hands. I found myself feeling helpless, knowing there was nothing more I could say or do. I knew God was in the car with us and heard everything. I can't explain it. It is just a knowing that God heard everything said and saw everything done. Psalms 139:7 says, "Where can I go from your Spirit? Where can I flee from your presence?" God hears everything and He knows what is in our hearts. He loves us and does everything He can to get our attention to help us. As I drove home, something stirred inside me.

three
HOLY SPIRIT INTERCEDES THROUGH US

Now I had thirty miles to drive home. I had such mixed emotions going on inside me. In the past two days, Steven shared with me while in a shaken state that an angel had chased after him yelling "Stop Steven, Stop!" He was desperate to find a place that could help him "really soon!" I had spent most of the day at work in my office making phone calls to locate a Teen Challenge treatment facility. I felt so fortunate to find one available that had an immediate opening. All my son had to do was make one phone call and say "yes." Now, driving home, I had an overwhelming urgency to get into the privacy of my home as quickly as I possibly could.

When I arrived home, I pulled my car into the garage. I had an eight-month-old puppy connected to a long leash secured in the middle of my garage while I was at work. While driving my car into the garage, this puppy got hung-up on the left side of my car causing his strap to break the side mirror off of my car. I could see as I drove into the garage that my puppy was excited to see me and was on the wrong side of my car wanting to greet me. This positioned the long strap over my car to break the mirror off. The puppy was okay, but my car had some damage.

This happened only because of the unusual urgency I felt inside me to get into my house. I couldn't get into my house fast enough. I didn't logically have anything on my mind driving me to get home in such a hurry. I was distraught over the conversation I had with Steven and hearing the words after he left my car that "he would be in heaven forever." I was so compelled to hurry home, not even thinking about what I would do there.

I safely unleashed my puppy and without thinking ran quickly into my house. Laying my purse and books from work down on the floor inside the door, I went into the kitchen. For some unknown reason, I turned on a CD player that was sitting on top of the refrigerator. I hardly ever used this CD player but remembered I had purchased a new song and had not listened to it yet. I pushed one button, and this song began to play. It began with soft sounds of beautiful bells chiming. Then LeAnn Squier, psalmist at Glory of Zion, Denton, Texas, softly sang, "Someone is going to hear from heaven, and it might as well be me."

When I heard this, without even thinking I dropped to the floor on my knees and cried out to God. I had a gush of deep emotions pour out to God from the most inner place of my being. I had no more words to speak to God regarding Steven's situation. What could I possibly say to God that would make any sense? God knows everything and sees everything and hears everything. I had no more words. Only heartfelt cries were coming out of me.

I had received the Baptism of the Holy Spirit many years earlier and would often pray in the Spirit. This is in 1 Corinthians 14:15, "I will pray with my spirit, but I will also pray with my mind, I will sing with my spirit, but I will also sing with my mind." So I cried out to God in this Holy Spirit language because there were no words of my own understanding that could verbalize what I was feeling deep inside me. I had never been so desperate that the only thing I could do was to fall on my knees and cry out for help. I could do nothing but pour out everything to God. I had no natural understanding about what was going on inside me, but there was such an intense urgency to get before God and cry out to Him.

Only the Holy Spirit inside me knew what this was all about. The Holy Spirit was praying through me on Steven's behalf.

The Baptism of the Holy Spirit gives you a prayer language. You speak out of your own spirit directly to the Spirit of God. If I would have verbalized my thoughts, my words would have sounded something like this: "We have been through two treatment centers, and they haven't worked. We have been through the courts of the legal system, and it has changed nothing. I relocated my home to provide a better environment for him, but that didn't work out. I don't know what more to do for my son. He refuses now to go to Teen Challenge, and I don't know what I can do."

This evening of crying out in prayer was all orchestrated by the Holy Spirit and the love of God for every soul, for Steven's soul. I raised my hands to God during this time as if giving this whole situation over to God. I asked God to please help us. I sensed the urgency that I was coming to God with my son's life. I had no words in English to communicate to God, just loud groans. The Holy Spirit communicates to God through us in these groanings. This type of prayer is in Romans 8:26 and 27: "In the same way, the Spirit helps us in our weakness. We do not know what we ought to pray for, but the Spirit Himself intercedes for us with groans that words cannot express. And he who searches our hearts knows the mind of the Spirit because the Spirit intercedes for the saints in accordance with God's will."

At one point in this time of crying out, I could sense with my being that I was in a heavenly place that I had not ever been before or ever seen before. I could see with my eyes of intercession, and I say it that way because my natural eyes were closed. I was in deep groaning and crying, but I could see with my eyes of intercession that I was entering into a conference room where there was a meeting or a type of convening being held. I knew that this conference room was behind God's courtroom. I could tell there were other conference rooms behind this courtroom. I felt I was brought here because it was important that I be in this place with these others. I do not know who the others were, but I knew it was about my son. I knew because of my intercession, I was able to be part of this. I know my intercession spoke in that room. Hebrews 4:16 says, "Let us then approach the throne of grace with confidence, so that we may receive mercy and find grace to help us in our time of need." I had no prior knowledge of any Court of Heaven teaching at this time. I was just crying out to God through the leading of the Holy Spirit. The Holy Spirit is our helper and counselor as we yield to Him.

Driving home that day, I did not know I would be praying like this. But I sensed something happening inside me because of the urgent feelings. I stayed on the floor for a long time crying out loudly to God. This cry came from the deepest parts of my belly for my son's life. When the urgency released and I had nothing left inside me, I got up from the floor and went to bed.

four
DECISIONS CAN MEAN LIFE OR DEATH

The next morning as I was preparing to go to work, I had a noticeable uneasiness inside me. I felt like something was very wrong. I could hardly focus while getting dressed. Feeling confused and even disoriented, I wondered if I should even go to work. With no valid reason to stay home other than something stirring inside me that I couldn't identify, I drove to my workplace. Leaving my car at a dealership to have the mirror repaired, I got a ride to my workplace. All morning I had difficulty concentrating in my office.

Just after the noon hour a police officer and a chaplain entered our office. They identified me as the one they needed to visit with. I had no idea why. My first thought was I may have opened a website that I should not have on my computer because having access to many software programs and sites. I really did not know why they came to see me.

We stepped across the hall into an empty office and all sat down at a table. The officer asked me if I had a son named Steven. I replied yes. Then the officer told me they found my son sleeping in a friend's garage on a couch. Then she told me that my son did not wake up this morning. I gasped in complete shock. No matter how difficult our situation is, we always think everything will be okay.

Now I understood what the officer had just said, and I understood why the chaplain was present with the officer. They were telling me my son had died. I got that message. But deep inside me, I didn't want to completely receive what they were saying because I wanted to have some faith, just a little bit of faith remaining inside of me to go to my son and pray for him to live. I did not tell the officer or the chaplain I wanted to go pray for him to live because they would have thought I was crazy. But I knew Matthew 10:8 that said, "Heal the sick, raise the dead, cleanse those who have leprosy, drive out demons, freely you have received, freely give."

I knew that believers of the Word of God could lay hands on the sick and they could be healed. I had seen people healed. This scripture also said we could lay hands on the dead and see them live. I had heard other people's testimonies of praying for loved ones that had died and they lived. I thought about Andrew Wommack's testimony about his son who had died. His son was already placed in a morgue when Andrew and his wife were notified. Andrew and his wife drove to where their son was, believing to pray for their son to live. They did pray and their son did come back to life. I had to at least have the opportunity to pray for Steven to live. I would not back away from what I knew about that Scripture. I was going to hold on to that little seed of faith inside me.

After the initial shock, I tried to stay calm and not fall apart because I wanted to hold on to a little piece of faith. I asked the officer where my son was and if I could go see him. The officer said he was at the Clay County Sheriff's office in a cooled vehicle. It is Minnesota's regulations that when a young person dies, they are automatically sent to Minneapolis for an autopsy for investigation purposes. The officer drove me to the car dealership where my car had been repaired.

Calling my other two children, I told them what had happened. My daughter came with me to the Sheriff's office. When we arrived an officer took us to the County vehicle where Stevie was. I climbed into the back of this cold vehicle and sat next to my son. I couldn't visually see him because of the body bag he was in due to the investigation. I laid my hands on him and I prayed softly. I spoke to Steven to come back to life. I spoke "life" to come back into him. Then I asked God to let Steven come back to us. I sat there quietly focused on listening to what God might be saying and not letting myself fall apart. I just wanted to hear what God was saying.

I was so thankful that I got to hear other people's testimonies before this event in my life. I heard them tell how they walked through the death of a loved one and stood in faith praying for them to live. Even after hours of being dead, they saw life came back into their loved one. These experiences shared by other people helped me to reach out to my son with the little bit of faith I had to speak life over him.

Because of hearing these testimonies, I was able to remain calm and have faith in praying for Steven. After a while, I sensed my son would not come back but was okay where he was. Then I remembered the day before, the still small voice that spoke after I had visited with Steven in my car. God spoke these words to me: "He wasn't going to go to church for the next year of his life, but he would be in heaven for eternity." God tells us things like this for our comfort. He is our Comforter. We don't know what the next day will bring. But God does. He is faithful to prepare us for it even when we don't realize that He is preparing us for it.

I then drove to the nursing facility where my mother was a resident. My father was visiting at the time. I sat with them and told them what had happened. All my father said was that I needed to purchase a burial plot at the cemetery and who I would need to contact. They were saddened but gave me logical direction on what I needed to do.

I met with the person in charge of the cemetery and purchased a plot. Then I contacted the funeral director in our small town to make an appointment to meet with them. In the evening, I sat with my other two children in my home. I had no comforting words to give them. We all just sat there in disbelief, numb, and hurting. The one thing I needed to hear was the comforting words "this wasn't my fault" because I felt it was.

I was feeling an overwhelming guilt, thinking of all the things I could have done differently or should have done to help my son more. I wish I would have stayed home from work more. Spent more time with him. I wish I would have hugged and kissed him more. I had the feeling that I did not help him enough. I should have been more kind and patient with him.

There are things we all could have done differently, but if we knew what they were, we would probably have done them. We only live and walk in what we know at the time. We can help people in life by praying for them, feeding them, providing shelter, or giving counsel, but at the end of all of this, we all make our own decisions for our lives. It is a false responsibility that causes us to think we have control over other people's choices.

A month later, we learned the investigation details of what had taken place with our son that evening.

five
GOD DOES INTERVENE IN OUR LIVES

After the investigation of Steven's death, his father and I met with the police department to learn what had happened the evening before. They told us that Steven and two of his friends were driving in Moorhead. A police officer pulled them over. Steven had several tablets of Methadone in his pocket. He swallowed all of these when they were pulled over by the officer. Steven was afraid of being searched and having the officer find these drugs in his possession. He knew they would arrest him for possession of drugs. This felony would put him in prison. The officer only questioned the driver after pulling their car over and then let the three boys continue on their way with no further delay.

The three boys then drove to Barnesville. Steven decided he would stay the night and sleep on the couch in his friend's garage. One of his friends wanted to take him to the emergency room because he felt Steven had taken too much Methadone. But Steven said no; he would be okay. This friend asked Steven several more times to go with him to the hospital, but Steven insisted he would be okay. He had lived through so many risky choices already. I'm sure he thought this one would be no different.

As time passed by, I could see God's hand of intervention in Steven's life. An angel came to warn him two days before. This angel was chasing after him, yelling at him, "Stop Steven, Stop!" Angels can be sent to warn us of impending dangers. This is found in Exodus 23:20, 21a: "See, I am sending an angel ahead of you to guard you along the way and to bring you to the place I have prepared. Pay attention to him and listen to what he says."

This happened just before I came to pick Steven up, so he could share with me what he had experienced. It is a testimony of God's goodness. God does send angels to minister to us and to help us: "Are not all angels ministering spirits sent to serve those who will inherit salvation?" (Hebrews 1:14).

The next day, God moved on me to intercede for

Steven just a few hours before an officer pulled their car over, when Steven swallowed these tablets of Methadone. It was the Holy Spirit that came upon me to pray and used me to intercede for Steven's soul and eternal life. Intercession is a prayer offered on behalf of another person. I didn't know what would happen, but God knew.

Even Steven had a sensing that he needed help "really soon." Steven told me several times in the previous days that he needed help "really soon." He was asking for help, but when it was offered to him, he didn't take it. He may have had the Methadone in his pocket while he was talking with me in the car. The voice in his pocket was louder than mine.

Steven's friend wanted to take him to the hospital. This friend asked him several times if he could take him to the hospital, and each time, Steven refused to go.

These are just the things I know of that show God intervened on Steven's behalf. He always intervenes on our behalf. God was probably doing other things to keep this from happening that I am not aware of. God is in the business of giving life and restoring lives. Even when God sees us making all the wrong choices, He will move upon someone to pray for us to make the right choice. God also moves upon us to pray for salvation for other people. Man's time on earth is only for a short period, but where we live for eternity is a very long time. Eternity is forever.

I believe God had good plans for Steven's life, and it wasn't in God's plan for him to leave us so soon. You can see God's mercy and love when He tries to get our attention and steer us in a better direction. God does care about our safety, and He is there to help us. I believe God is always talking to us. We just need to recognize that it is His voice and then respond appropriately to Him.

Tragedies like these can literally break our hearts.

six

MY BROKEN-HEARTED CONDITION

Even though I could recognize God's goodness and urgency in getting Steven's attention those last few days, because of overwhelming grief and sadness, I would still cry every night for one, two, or three hours before going to bed. I continued to grieve over the loss of his life and of dreams that would never be realized. I felt guilt for not being a "better mom." I also felt the pain, the grief, and the brokenness of my other two children. This added to all my pain.

I read every book and listened to every CD teaching I could find about overcoming grief. Some teachings were by Bill and Janet Sudduth, who had a healing and deliverance ministry out of Colorado. Any other material I could find on healing and deliverance of grief, I sought it out. I did every kind of prophetic act and every kind of symbolic act I could think of to close the door to this sadness and grief inside me. Grief isn't something you can go to the doctor and have surgically removed. It affects our emotions and our mind, which comprise our soul. It can also lodge deeper into the heart affecting our spirit. This is why I sought spiritual healing and deliverance, also known as inner healing, through books and other material.

I had a difficult time when shopping at the grocery store where I had routinely gone in previous years with my children. I would cry when I saw items on the shelves in the grocery store that Steven liked and would pick out to eat. The grocery store was the most difficult public place to go because of my memories of him there. It seemed like yesterday he was a little guy, sitting in the shopping cart.

A couple of years after this, I realized I was still stuck in grief and in an emotionally unhealthy place. I would cry easily almost every night. Not knowing how to get past this continuous grief, I became concerned about myself. Antidepressants only alleviate symptoms; they don't deal with the root of the problem. They don't change the way we think or how we handle certain situations. Therefore, I didn't resort to taking prescription medication.

As a precaution, I scheduled an appointment to have a physical examination. Afterward, they told me that my heart function was only 57% and my adrenal glands were at a low functioning level. Again I was given a prescription for an antidepressant but didn't purchase them. Right or wrong, that was just how I handled that. I felt my problem of being stuck in grief had become a spiritual problem because it had gone unresolved for a long time.

I realized I would need to take active steps in choosing to come out of this grief. I knew I was still feeling guilty or somewhat responsible for my son's drug addiction and overdose. I talked to God about this whole situation and had repented for all of my mistakes in raising my children. Yet, the guilt would not leave me. I couldn't stop feeling guilty and responsible. By now, I wanted to accept what had happened and try to continue on with my life.

I began taking some natural supplements for my heart and for my adrenal glands. I began attending a Bible fellowship that believed in praying for the sick and seeing God's love heal people. I began asking God to heal my heart. It was about this time that I saw an advertisement on television about broken heart syndrome. They said it was an actual medical condition recognized by the Mayo Clinic called "Takotsubo Cardiomyopathy" or "Broken Heart Syndrome."[2]

This type of heart condition affects mostly women

over the age of 50. It is usually reversed without any difficulty. The name Takotsubo comes from a Japanese Octopus trap.[3] It was given this name because it affected the left ventricle of the heart, taking on the same shape as that of an octopus trap. It has a balloon shape with a narrowing at the entrance. I enjoyed studying things out and noting information like this. God sometimes speaks to us to give us keys to spiritual truths.

In the Bible, a part of Isaiah 61 says, "He has sent me to bind up the brokenhearted." This means that the Lord heals the brokenhearted. In this Scripture, the Greek meaning of broken-hearted is *grief, to destroy or crush*.[4] The Hebrew meaning for broken-hearted is *shattering, dashed to pieces or broken to shivers*.[5]

According to Isaiah 61, Jesus' mission in coming to earth was to restore us to a right relationship with God our Father and bring healing to the brokenhearted. We become brokenhearted when there is a loss in our lives, such as a death, loss of a job, a divorce or even if we are feeling unloved. There must be a lot of people who have a brokenness in their hearts or God would not have written Isaiah 61 as one purpose of Christ's coming to earth. Brokenhearted people are on God's mind.

The complete chapter of Isaiah 61 reads like this:
> The Spirit of the Sovereign Lord is on me, because the Lord has anointed me to preach good news to the poor. He has sent me to bind

up the brokenhearted, to proclaim freedom for the captives and release from darkness for the prisoners, to proclaim the year of the Lord's favor and the day of vengeance of our God, to comfort all who mourn, and provide for those who grieve in Zion, to bestow on them a crown of beauty instead of ashes, the oil of gladness instead of mourning, and a garment of praise instead of a spirit of despair. They will be called oaks of righteousness, a planting of the Lord for the display of his splendor. They will rebuild the ancient ruins and restore the places long devastated; they will renew the ruined cities that have been devastated for generations. Aliens will shepherd your flocks; foreigners will work your fields and vineyards. And you will be called priests of the Lord, you will be named ministers of our God. You will feed on the wealth of nations, and in their riches, you will boast. Instead of their shame my people will receive a double portion, and instead of disgrace they will rejoice in their inheritance; and so they will inherit a double portion in their land and everlasting joy will be theirs. (Isaiah 61)

God wants to give us life instead of death, joy instead of sadness. God also wants us to have a full life while we are here on earth. John 10:10, "The thief comes only to steal and kill and destroy; I have come that they may have life, and have it to the full."

God wants to restore the broken places in our lives.

seven

GRIEVING CAUSES HEALTH ISSUES

A few years after my son's death, I experienced a couple situations where people's lives were falling apart due to health issues possibly related to grieving over the loss of their children. One such example occurred when I had taken my sister-in-law to her dialysis appointment in Grand Forks, North Dakota. While sitting in the waiting room for several hours, I visited with another woman whose husband was receiving dialysis. This woman shared with me that ever since their adult son had died in a car accident her husband's health had been declining.

Only a few months prior, she and her husband were in a vehicle following their son, who was driving a vehicle just ahead of them, when their son swerved to miss hitting something lying on the road. He was ejected from his car. The woman explained that both she and her husband saw the whole accident occur, which was traumatic for them. After the accident was over, they stopped their car and ran to their son's lifeless body. They called 911. An ambulance arrived, but it was evident their son did not survive the accident.

After this event, the father began having breathing difficulties at night while trying to sleep. Then he began having fluttering of his heart. This wife explained that her husband's health kept declining until now his kidneys were not functioning and he was having dialysis. In just a few short months, her husband had gone from a healthy man to having almost all of his bodily organs malfunction, and the doctors had no medical explanation for.

When a traumatic event happens, there can be a shattering in a person's bodily systems. This shattering can cause a person's hormones to go out of balance. It can compromise their chemical balance of serotonin and dopamine levels along with all other chemicals and hormones in the body. Traumatic events can even cause a shock to one's bodily organs to where they have difficulty functioning properly, which in turn affects other organs in the body. If this trauma is not relieved or reversed in the body, then there will be some failure of functioning that could be life-threatening.

Another example I witnessed was when I volunteered as a Spiritual Caregiver at a hospital in Fargo, North Dakota. My role was to visit families in waiting rooms and share light conversation with them. I would ask them if they needed anything, or offer to pray with them if they wanted me to. One day, I was in the Intensive Care Unit (ICU) family waiting room visiting with a woman whose husband was having a heart procedure that day while in ICU. She told me much of their history leading up to this time.

She stated two years earlier her husband's daughter, who was her step-daughter, was killed in a house fire. Since then, her husband's health had declined. He had begun having heart problems. His health continued to spiral until they were not expecting him to survive. That day the doctors were trying a certain procedure on his heart, but there was a very small chance that it would help him.

This is what grief does to people. I believe this is the effect of a broken heart. It puts a stress on people's bodies that their heart and other organs cannot possibly manage. A traumatic situation can shatter the body's systems. It causes grief to come into a person. If the person does not recognize the grief and process it healthily, with the help of others, and then remove it through prayer or some other means, it will crush the person's heart and destroy their overall health.

It is difficult to lose the people we love, and it causes us to grieve because it alters the way we live when they are no longer with us. But we cannot let it destroy our lives also. I am convinced that only God can heal a broken heart.

eight
TRAUMA AND GRIEF

Traumatic experiences result from highly stressful events that shatter a person's sense of safety, security, and serenity. In many cases, trauma renders a person helpless and vulnerable, hardened and volatile in a world perceived as dangerous. In many cases, traumatic experiences include a threat to life or overall well-being. Any situation that leaves a person feeling overwhelmed and alone can be traumatic, even if it doesn't involve physical harm. The more anxious, panicky and paralyzed a person feels, the more likely that person has been traumatized.

Grieving and deep disappointment can be very difficult. It feels impossible to see a way back to wholeness. When a horrible event happens in a life, it affects us deeply. We probably weren't able to deal with the trauma when it happened because it was so shocking and overwhelming. We had to stuff most of the trauma down inside just so we could carry out our daily functions. But the trauma we stuffed down inside creates problems for us.

Somehow we have to pull that trauma out of our soul and spirit so the wound it created inside can heal. If we never remove the trauma that covers the wound in our heart, we will never be able to heal. This will then become who we are, a person who is broken and hurting inside. What is in our hearts, whether it is joy or pain, will be seen on us externally.

I could recognize that I was stuck in grief. I knew it was not healthy for grief to linger on me as long as it had. Having been in the medical field and also having read a lot of books on inner healing, I understood that my heart had been shattered and wounded. After a period of several years, it was affecting my emotions and my ability to think clearly.

Years earlier, when I was a nurse, I had seen people healed when praying for them. I had witnessed God's love heal people. I had recognized and literally seen demonic spirits and cast them out of people and out of my home. I had seen angels on several occasions. I did not seek these experiences. I was just reading my Bible, wanting to know God, and seeking to love the

Lord with all of my heart. Then over a long period of difficult situations, and now my son's death, it seemed everything in my life was falling apart. Here I was, sort of a mess, trying to come out of grief and recover myself back to a state of normalcy.

I wanted to be healed of the sadness and brokenness I felt inside. I didn't know how to bring reconciliation to this wide spectrum of events in my life. Years earlier I witnessed other people healed by sharing God's love with them. For the last ten years I was experiencing the difficulties of divorce and now losing my son's life in an overdose.

While wanting to get help for myself, I was also deeply crying out to the Lord about where I could go to be mentored and possibly receive the truth of God's Word about praying for the sick. I also needed help in coming out of grief and recovering my own health and my own life.

I always desired to have a mentor in a healing school but had never found one where I lived. I always wanted a setting where I could study the Bible, especially healing, and experience praying for the sick alongside other people.

In praying about it and crying out to God for answers to all my questions, I was desperate enough to move somewhere, anywhere. I took out a map of the United States and told God I would go anywhere to receive Biblical truth about my life and circumstances, so I could come out of grief and set out on the life-course God had planned for me.

I knew of several healing and deliverance ministries from taking some Biblical online courses. I identified where they were on the map. I could retire from my job but would need to continue earning income after relocating. It seemed like a huge risk to move away. I had the security of a good job and living at my beautiful home in the country with no financial debt. Yet I was living in deep grief over the loss of a loved one's life and had a sense of not pursuing the longings God had placed inside me.

nine
CRYING OUT FOR ANSWERS

How do people recover wholeness after trauma and grief? I admit I am far from being an expert or even knowledgeable on this subject. Sometimes all God asks us to do is share our experience. I don't have all the answers, but I know the One who does. For years I asked God for answers to my many questions.

I came to the place that I would risk everything I had to even begin to heal the brokenness I felt in my heart. We can find this deep desire to risk everything for something meaningful in Mark 8:36, 37. "What good is it for a man to gain the whole world, yet forfeit his soul? Or what can a man give in exchange for his soul?" To me, this meant I could have a great job, a beautiful place to live, and no financial debt, yet remain stuck in this place of deep grief and sadness and never experience life. I was willing to risk it all to follow a longing inside me whereby I could become healed from being brokenhearted and possibly have a more meaningful purpose for my life.

To help me make *this* decision of if I should relocate and if so, where, I remembered reading long ago in Bishop Bill Hamon's book, *Prophets and Personal Prophecy*, that when a person is making important life decisions, he or she should have God's Word, God's Will, and God's Way.[6] God's Word and Will should be fairly easy to identify in your life. I could identify these two elements in my life. The long-time desire I had to be mentored in praying for the sick was supported in the Bible. This was God's Word. The desperate need I had to be healed of grieving was God's Will. But the third element, God's Way, is more difficult and time-consuming. These three elements need to be answered before making major decisions.

The promises and inward drive I had from the Lord seemed to support God's Will for me to pursue this adventure. I had several prophetic words and scriptures that were close to my heart that supported God's Word to relocate and be mentored by a church that prays for the sick. But it took time to pray and work out God's Way to make this transition. I wasn't sure where

I would go or my whole purpose in moving other than being healed of a broken heart and mentored in praying for the sick.

I owned my home and needed to decide if I should sell now or rent it out or leave it empty to see how this adventure works out for me. I had to decide when I would leave my workplace to give a proper notice. I would need to complete the transfer of my nursing license in case I decided to pursue nursing employment after relocating. So the "Way" took more planning.

With a large map laid out before me, I located potential ministries and churches that taught on praying for the sick and where I could find my own answers for healing my heart. For many days I would look at this map and ask God if I should go, and if so, where I should go. Then one day, I heard within myself the name "Bill Hamon." It surprised me a little because Bill Hamon's church was not one I had identified on my map. Although I had many books by him and had heard him and the different ones from his church speak throughout the years when they came into my area. But I heard his name so clearly that there was no question God was speaking to move there.

I didn't even know where this church was, so I had to research that out. It was in Florida. I knew nothing about this area. I lived in the far northern part of the United States and God was asking me to move to the most southern part of the United States. I was sure I heard this clearly, yet I was still waiting for confirmation. In 2 Corinthians 13:1, it says "This will be my third visit to you. 'Every matter must be established by the testimony of two or three witnesses.'" God even says He confirms His Word to us with two or three witnesses.

The first witness I received on relocating to Florida was while I was at work. A patient came up to me out of nowhere and for no reason other than to ask me if I was from Florida. Of course, I told him I was not. But he insisted he had seen me there. This happened just after I heard God tell me to move to Florida. Well, I set it aside as a possible coincidence.

My second witness came while working on a computer in my office. I accidentally pulled up a screen view of the Emerald Coast of Florida. The aerial view really caught my attention, showing the beautiful blue waters and white sand. I thought to myself, "that would surely be a beautiful place to live." I had no idea how that screen came up on my computer because I had not been searching for anything like this, nor did I even have on my mind anything of this nature.

The third witness came when I noticed in my home all three of my children over the last several years had each given me something pertaining to the ocean. One gave me a seashell treasure chest for a gift several years ago. Another gave me a seashell light ornament several years ago for a Christmas gift. Another gave me a large white seashell. I had never been to an ocean and now thought it strange how they had all given me something from the ocean. When they gave me these items, I am sure they had no intention or motive behind it. God can speak through anyone, and they may not even realize it.

I was volunteering as a Spiritual Caregiver at a hospital a couple of days a week after I would get off work from my day job. I had done this for three years. I loved doing this because I wanted opportunities to pray for the sick. I would mostly just visit in the family rooms until one day the administrator requested I visit the patient's rooms. I would begin on the top floor, visiting all the rooms, and then work my way to the bottom floor. This was a stretch for me to socialize with people whom I didn't know. I had no idea what the situation would be when I walked into the patient's room. I would introduce myself and make small talk, then offer to pray with them before leaving. Sometimes the nurses would direct me to a room with a patient who desired company.

One day they asked me to visit a young grandmother who had many health issues but was eager to talk. I asked her if I could pray for the healing of some of her issues. She said "Yes" and named off all of her problems. They were serious health problems and really stretched my faith. But then she showed me her feet while lying in bed. Her one foot came only to the top of her ankle on the other leg. It looked like her one foot was three or four inches shorter than the other foot. I had seen legs grow out just a little before, but this leg was exceptionally shorter than the other. Compared to all her other health issues, however, this was the one I had the most faith for, so I offered to pray for her leg to grow out to its normal length. This patient was more than happy to have me pray for her.

I held both her feet in my hands and spoke to the shorter leg to grow out to normal length, and it began to slowly move downward. It didn't stop moving until it had reached the same length as her other foot. Then they were both even. We both watched them grow out. We were both shocked at what had happened! As she sat up in bed, she told me her life story and how difficult it had been. She was from Florida and came for a short stay. A couple of nurses came into the room to perform some tests for this patient, so they asked me to step out of the room.

In all the time of coming to this hospital praying for the sick, this was the most evident healing or miracle I had seen. I was so excited at what God had done for her. I believed it wasn't by chance this woman was from Florida and was another confirmation that I needed to move there. Now I was being convinced that God was relocating me. Some of these things could just have been coincidences. But I was asking the Lord to speak to me about this decision, and I felt He was. I had hopes of receiving my own healing from grief and to also experience an atmosphere where I could be mentored in praying for the sick.

A few months later, I relocated to Florida to attend Bill Hamon's church and to attend their Bible college during the day while working a full-time job during the night. As I continued on this new journey, my heart began to heal. I was receiving healing ministry and prayer. Life was being spoken in to me from the prophetic ministry at this church. I could hear God's voice more clearly because the overwhelming guilt I had carried for so long was now leaving me. I was having a more positive interaction with people and could release the grip that grief had on me.

God was answering my questions one at a time, which brought me comfort. Through the Biblical classroom studies, and through the healing and prophetic ministry I received at this church, the layers of guilt were being removed from me. I was receiving God's love for me. This all helped me to untangle my wrong way of thinking and to rightly see some of the difficulties I had experienced. This all helped to remove the grief I had carried. My heart was becoming whole.

There were some changes I needed to make to remove the negative effects that this particular traumatic event had on me. For me, it was a geographic move and a complete lifestyle change. For others, it could be as simple as taking better care of yourself by getting more rest and eating a better diet. Friends and family around us can offer emotional support that help us through these difficult experiences. There are many good resources, such as books, music, or a new hobby that can bring comfort to people when dealing with a stressful experience. God knows what you need. Ask Him questions, and He will answer you.

Jeremiah 29:12, 13 says, "Then you will call upon me and come and pray to me, and I will listen to you. You will seek me and find me when you seek me with all your heart." I cried out for some answers to my questions about my painful crushed feelings surrounding my son's death. I took one step at a time in walking out this transition of relocating and living a different lifestyle which helped release my answers.

Now I was asking the Lord, "What about my future?" Jeremiah 29:11 says, "'For I know the plans I have for you,' declares the Lord, 'plans to prosper you and not to harm you, plans to give you hope and a future.'" What are His plans for me now? Is there any way a loss can be turned around into something good? Isaiah 61 is the "Turn it Around" chapter in the Bible.

ten

TURN IT AROUND

Isaiah 61 is a scripture that has always been close to my heart even when I didn't completely understand it. I am still in the process of understanding it. Jesus' mission in coming to earth was to restore us to a right relationship with God our Father and to bring healing to the brokenhearted.

We restore our relationship with God by choosing to give Him our heart and life, then daily walking that out. We let God heal our broken heart by hearing the truth of God's Word and applying it to our lives. Knowing the truth allows the Spirit of God to remove the pain in our heart and allows us to receive His love. This is stated in John 8:32: "Then you will know the truth, and the truth will set you free." All of this brings inner healing to the brokenhearted. Isaiah 61:3 says, "and provide for those who grieve in Zion, to bestow on them a crown of beauty instead of ashes, the oil of gladness instead of mourning, and a garment of praise instead of a spirit of despair."

I can't change anything, but God can. He hears us when we talk to Him and when we make our requests known to Him. He is also a God of justice. This is in Isaiah 61:8: "For I, the Lord, love justice; I hate robbery and iniquity. In my faithfulness I will reward them and make an everlasting covenant with them." Sickness, disease, and premature death are an injustice because they take life away from us. Generational alcoholism, divorce, hopelessness, strife, and drug overdoses are all injustices. They all rob, steal, and destroy life. Jesus came to give us life. He paid for our sins with His blood on the cross so we could be saved. Luke 19:10 says, "For the Son of Man came to seek and to save what was lost." The word "saved" here means *to deliver or protect, to heal, preserve, save, do well, and be (make) whole.*[7]

Many years ago, I established in my heart that God was good and is the giver of life and that He was not the author of sickness, disease, accidents, or premature death. He is not the one that causes these things to happen, nor does He desire these things to happen to us. But He promises to be with us and to walk with us throughout our lives if we ask Him to.

Many years earlier, I was not able to carry my first child full-term and lost him at six months gestation. For the loss of his life, I asked God for a bounty of one million souls to come into heaven and to be saved from eternal hell. Genesis 4:10 says the innocent blood cries out from the ground for vindication: "The Lord said, "What have you done? Listen! Your brother's blood cries out to me from the ground." This scripture says innocent blood cries out for vindication. God is the one who vindicates. This is in Psalm 135:14, "For the Lord will vindicate his people and hae compassion on his servants." In the midst of my sadness over the loss of that baby, I chose to set my heart to love and to know Jesus Christ more. I knew God would honor my prayer for one million souls. At that time, in the privacy of my home, I prayed for people to be saved. This was the only way I knew to turn something bad into something good.

When the life of my second son, Stevie, was lost, I asked God for the same thing, a bounty of another million souls.

In 2017, I read the book *Touching Heaven* by Dr. Chauncey Crandall. He tells about his experience of losing his young son's life to Leukemia. After his son died, Dr. Crandall stated in his book, "I want a million souls for my son!"[8] He verbalized that his son had been martyred by the evil of cancer and exhorted the

Lord to let him see a bounty of souls brought into His kingdom in exchange for his son's life.[9] I could hardly believe what I was reading in his book. I cried when I read that.

My asking God for one million souls for each of my son's lives was not anything I had ever shared with anyone. There was no reason to share it with anyone. When I read Dr. Crandall had done the same thing, I was so surprised! I had never heard anyone else say this. God was letting me know I was not the only one asking for this certain request and that He had heard me.

Dr. Crandall shared in his book that after his son had passed away, he had to make a decision, at a time that his heart was breaking; would he turn away from loving God, or would he turn to Him in a time of loss?[10] We all may be faced with that decision at some point in our lives. God is not the author of sickness and disease or premature death. God has good plans for our lives and wants to fully work with us to help us fulfill them. We may not understand everything while we are here on earth, but we can ask those questions one day in heaven. Meanwhile, be encouraged to set your heart to love God and to seek Him: "And without faith it is impossible to please God, because anyone who comes to Him must believe that He exists and that He rewards those who earnestly seek Him" (Hebrews 11:6).

No greater event can happen to a person than to be born again into the Kingdom of God and have eternal salvation. When you know that a loved one has gone to heaven when they pass away, you can be so thankful for that. If you have Eternal Life living inside of you, then you will see them again one day. We can have the hope of talking with them and being with them again: "Brothers, we do not want you to be ignorant about those who fall asleep or to grieve like the rest of men, who have no hope. We believe that Jesus died and rose again and so we believe that God will bring with Jesus those who have fallen asleep in Him" (1 Thessalonians 4:13,14).

Eternal life is obtained only through accepting Jesus Christ as your Savior. Do you have Eternal Life inside of you? If you died tonight, do you know for sure that you would be in heaven?

If you do not know Jesus Christ as your Savior, I would like to invite you to give your heart and your life to Him now. You only need to ask Jesus into your life and receive Him. He will make your life meaningful and whole while you live on earth and give you eternal life with Him when you die.

Dear Lord Jesus, I come to You now.
Forgive me for my sins. Come into my heart.
I want You as my Lord and as my Savior.
Thank You, Jesus, for paying my debt of sin with Your blood.

Thank You for loving me and saving me.
Thank You for walking with me from this day forward.

If you have lost a loved one's life prematurely, I would like to pray with you.

Heavenly Father, you see this one who is praying with me right now. You know everything about what has caused them to grieve. You now everything about the circumstance and situation surrounding the loss of their loved one's life, their child's life, or their brother or sister's life. Lord, I know this has grieved Your heart also because you had plans for them. I ask you, Lord, to put your arms around this one who is praying with me. Hold them. Love them. Remove from them the grief, the pain, and the sadness of the traumatic experience they endured in losing this one whom they loved. Let them feel the great tangible love that You have for them. I ask that You would heal their broken heart and make them whole in their mind and in their emotions. Give them Your peace. Let them know what Your plan and will are for their life. Be with them and help them each day. In Jesus' name. Amen.

ENDNOTES

1 *Prophet's and Personal Prophecy* Copyright 1987 by Destiny Image Publishers P.O. Box 310 Shippensburg, PA 17257-0310 pg 32
2 https://www.jstage.jst.go.jp/article/circj/78/9/78_CJ-14-0859/_html
3 https://www.health.harvard.edu/heart-health/takotsubo-cardiomyopathy-broken-heart-syndrome
4 *The Strongest Strong's Exhaustive Concordance of the Bible*, by James Strong, LL.D. ST.D. Copyright 2001 by Zondervan, Grand Rapids, Michigan 49530 ISBN 978-0-310-23343-5
5 Ibid
6 *Prophets and Personal Prophecy* Copyright 1987 by Destiny Image Publishers P.O. Box 310 Shippensburg, PA 17257-0310
7 *The Strongest Strong's Exhaustive Concordance of the Bible*, by James Strong, LL.D. ST.D. Copyright 2001 by Zondervan, Grand Rapids, Michigan 49530 ISBN 978-0-310-23343-5
8 *Touching Heaven* copyright 2015 by Chauncey W. Crandall VI, M.D. FaithWords Hachette Book Group, Inc.1290 Avenue of the American, New York, NY 10104 978-1-4555-6278-7 pg 184
9 Ibid
10 Ibid

BIBLIOGRAPHY

Books

1. All Scripture is taken from Thompson Chain-Reference Bible New International Version Copyright 1990 by The B.B. Kirkbride Bible Company, Inc. Indianapolis, Indiana
2. The Strongest Strong's Exhaustive Concordance of the Bible, by James Strong, LL.D. ST.D. Copyright 2001 by Zondervan, Grand Rapids, Michigan 49530 ISBN 978-0-310-23343-5
3. Touching Heaven copyright 2015 by Chauncey W. Crandall VI, M.D. FaithWords Hachette Book Group, Inc.1290 Avenue of the American, New York, NY 10104
4. Prophets and Personal Prophecy Copyright 1987 by Destiny Image Publishers P.O. Box 310 Shippensburg, PA 17257-0310

Websites

1. https://www.health.harvard.edu/heart-health/takotsubo-cardiomyopathy-broken-heart-syndrome
2. https://www.jstage.jst.go.jp/article/circj/78/9/78_CJ-14-0859/_html

MORE FROM THE AUTHOR

GOD, WHAT IS MY BABY'S NAME?

Because of the shame and guilt a woman and man experience when there is an abortion, they grieve in silence. There is nowhere to go to have this pain removed. The medical field can perform all kinds of marvelous things for our bodies, but there is only one that can heal the pain of a broken heart. That Great Physician's name is Jesus Christ.

REVEALING GOD'S TRUTH ON ABORTION

A Study Guide to *God, What is My Baby's Name?*
"Whether you are a woman who has suffered in silence over a past abortion, a family member or friend with a loved one who has had an abortion, or a pastor or counselor, this book will provide insight, strategy and a practical process to help restore hope and wholeness to broken lives."
- Jane Hamon

FIVE SMOOTH STONES TO SLAY INTIMIDATION

God does not send us into battle without weapons. He has given us five smooth stones just like He gave to David to use against Goliath, the voice of intimidation that wants to rise up in our lives. We do not ever have to be intimidated or shut down again. Know your identity and authority God has given you. Walk in the love and grace from God that causes us to overcome all obstacles. Secure your smooth stone of humility that says, "I trust you Lord." With these five smooth stones in your sling of faith, you will slay the voice of intimidation in your life.

WHAT KIND OF LOVE IS THIS?

Susan gave her life to Jesus during a Billy Graham television program. Later while working in a nursing home, she gained a burden to pray for the sick. She witnessed legs grow out, addictions leave, hips calcify causing patients to come off long-term bedrest, and a dementia patient begin to have a clear mind again. The pursuit of praying for the sick became her life ambition. Build your faith and unlock miracles on this incredible journey of the supernatural.

FOR SPEAKING ENGAGEMENTS OR QUESTIONS,
E-MAIL SUSANMARIEPENDER@GMAIL.COM.